Contents

Acknowledgements

Heather Birchall & Amelia Yeates

M any people have been involved in the realisation of this project. First of all, thanks must be given to the AAH for agreeing to finance the publication of these guidelines. Secondly, we would like to thank all the contributors: Dr Colin Cruise, Ivor Heal, Professor Catherine Karkov, Dr Outi Remes, and Dr Leslie Topp. They have all been extremely generous in sharing their experiences of exhibition planning and design, and their insightful comments form a large part of this publication. Thanks also go to Dr Laura MacCulloch for co-writing the main part of the guidelines text, to Mike Davies for securing and conducting the interviews, and to the Committee of the AAH Museums & Exhibitions Members Group for assistance and comments.

We would also like to take this opportunity to thank again the speakers who contributed to the event at University of Leeds in 2009 entitled Don't Ask for the Mona Lisa: Exhibitions Collaborations between Academics and Art Galleries. The experiences of the following academics and curators were shared with a lively audience, and valuable information was taken for this publication: Dr Patricia Allmer, Edwin Becker, Dr Gemma Blackshaw, Professor David Hill, Professor David Jackson, Professor Catherine Karkov, Dr Christiana Payne, May Redfern, and Ellen Tait.

Finally, we would like to acknowledge Donato Esposito who, at the AAH session out of which this project arose, shared his experiences. His warning to the assembled delegates forms the title of this publication.

September 2011

© copyright Association of Art Historians (AAH)

ISBN: 978-0-9571477-0-6

Published in 2012 by The Association of Art Historians (AAH)
70 Cowcross Street
London EC1M 6EJ
www.aah.org.uk

Registered Charity No. 282579

Copy editing, design, and layout: Jannet King edbulletin@aah.org.uk
Printed by The Print House, Brighton, Tel: 01273 325667

Cover illustrations: Marie Therese-Mayne

Introduction

Heather Birchall

The writing and publication of these guidelines was prompted by an event held by the Committee of the Museums & Exhibition Members Group of the Association of Art Historians (AAH), at the AAH Annual Conference at Manchester Metropolitan University in 2009. The session, entitled Curators Don't Bite, attracted a large crowd of academics and museum professionals eager to hear about the experiences, both positive and negative, of other academics and curators who had organised exhibitions. Following the event, it was clear that there was a demand for some advice on how to propose exhibitions and, once a show had been agreed, the practicalities of working with curators and other museum staff. This publication therefore aims to provide an introduction to key aspects of exhibition curation, from the early planning stages to the design and opening of the show.

Of course, every exhibition is different and, whilst this document cannot cover every aspect of exhibition planning, it does provide assistance to those organising both small-scale and large exhibitions, as well as offering guidance on working with paintings, sculptures, and contemporary installations. Whether your exhibition is to be held at a large venue, such as Tate Britain, with a team of curators, conservators, and technicians, or a smaller institution with only one or two members of staff, the intention of the authors has been to outline the possible eventualities and responsibilities associated with exhibition planning.

The first part of this publication gives guidance on why and how to propose an exhibition, and offers general advice on exhibition planning and installation. It describes the roles performed by certain staff members in galleries and museums, and the responsibilities they carry when an exhibition is being put together. Some technical terms are highlighted in bold in the main text, and defined in the margin.

The second part comprises case studies by academics who have worked on exhibitions for both large organisations, such as Birmingham Museum and Art Gallery, and small venues, including the Henry Moore Institute. This section also includes an interview with an exhibition designer that sets out some of the demands of fitting the design around the show's theme, and sheds light on how to create a space that doesn't overwhelm the exhibits.

At a time when museums and galleries are constantly tightening their budgets, a page at the end of this publication includes a list of funders to be approached if the museum's budget cannot cover all the costs associated with the show, such as producing a catalogue or organising an associated study day or conference.

Although the publication is primarily aimed at academics, and also freelances and students who may be considering putting together an exhibition proposal, we hope that it will also be useful for curators in the early stages of their careers working in a museum or gallery.

Proposing, Planning, and Installing an Exhibition

Heather Birchall and Laura MacCulloch

Putting together an exhibition is an extremely rewarding process, and this section offers advice on how to approach an institution and, following approval of an application, the steps that need to be taken in collaboration with the museum staff there.

It is hoped that, while discouraging you from requesting the *Mona Lisa*, this section will advise you how to take the necessary steps to secure the objects you desire, and create the exhibition which can bring your research to a new audience.

There are many benefits to organising an exhibition, some of which are:

♦ To make your area of research more widely known. Although you may have a specific age or social group in mind, museum exhibitions generally attract diverse audiences and, when your exhibition opens, your research will be firmly in the public realm. A good exhibition often encourages further discussion on the topic.

♦ To promote collaboration between museum professionals and academics. The Arts and Humanities Research Council (AHRC), in particular, are keen to promote such collaborations, and funding opportunities may be available.

♦ Professional development, including the experience of working with 'real' objects, artists, meeting museum professionals, and applying for funding.

♦ As most exhibitions are accompanied by catalogues or books, organising an exhibition usually provides opportunities to publish.

♦ Impact: in recent times, funding bodies and research councils have placed increasing emphasis on the idea of 'impact', i.e. that research should have some demonstrable impact, in economic or social terms, on the wider community, beyond academia. Conveying your research through an exhibition can be one way of achieving this.

Types of Exhibition

There are two main types of exhibition. The first, 'permanent', refers to exhibitions that run for up to 20 years, and are planned for galleries reserved specifically for this purpose, such as the National Gallery's main galleries. In addition, many museums and galleries have temporary exhibition spaces. 'Temporary' exhibitions usually run for between six weeks and six months. This document will largely focus on temporary exhibitions.

Things to Consider

Remuneration: National museums may pay a fee to guest curators, though this is unlikely to be much. Smaller organisations often only cover expenses and provide in-kind support, such as training and a work station.

If you are working on an exhibition for a museum or gallery affiliated with the university you are working for, you should not expect to receive a fee.

Time: Note that organising even a quick project to focus your research, or any small display, can be incredibly time-consuming, and there will be numerous demands on your time throughout the process.

Impact For more information on AHRC and Impact, see presentation by Professor Shearer West: www.ahrc.ac.uk/News/Events/Documents/armaimpact.pdf

The various forms an exhibition might take are:

Thematic: Here, a theme is the original concept, for example War and Medicine held at the Wellcome Collection in 2008, or Deep Rooted: How Trees Shape our Lives at the Whitworth Art Gallery, University of Manchester in 2009.

Retrospective/single artist: Usually works are chosen by a single artist whose career is being surveyed. There has been a tendency, for example, to hold a retrospective towards the end of an artist's career, or to celebrate the centenary of their birth, as with Tate Britain's Henry Moore exhibition held in 2010.

Interactive/immersive: This implies that the display depends for its effect on the visitor's contribution. Some art forms such as live art require audience participation.

Web-based: Online, or virtual, exhibitions are becoming increasingly common, although they can be as time-consuming as other types of show, and costs for copyright and image reproduction can be steep. Often galleries will hold an online exhibition alongside an actual display as a way of giving visitors more information than would be possible in the gallery itself.

> **Online exhibitions**
> See the British Library's London: A Life in Maps for a good example of an online exhibition.

Commissioning new work for an exhibition: There are a range of different types of permanent and temporary commissions that include a new work as part of an exhibition or season. Commissions may celebrate a specific event or the theme of a wider project. They may also develop the organisation's existing collection, while public art commissions are site-specific in the physical public domain, usually outside and accessible to all. Artists are commonly sourced from an open call for proposals, a long list of artists who are invited by curators, or a selection panel to submit a proposal. Many contemporary art residencies also include a commission of new work that is showcased at the end of the residency. These residencies have strong curatorial input and often support the development of the resident artist.

> **Commissions**
> Further information at:
> www.axisweb.org/atatcl.aspx?aid=612

Which Institution Should I Approach?

The main types of venue you might approach are:

National organisations: There are a total of 19 national museums in England, Scotland, Wales, and Northern Ireland. They house collections of national importance, and are wholly or mainly funded by the government. Examples include Tate, the National Gallery, National Museums Liverpool (which includes the Walker Art Gallery and the Lady Lever Art Gallery), and National Museums Scotland.

Local authority: Many city, county, and district councils operate some form of museum service. These museums are often run as part of a larger council department, such as leisure services, and vary greatly in size, from Manchester Art Gallery to Buckinghamshire County Museum, Aylesbury, and the William Morris Gallery, Walthamstow. Local authority museums may also operate over multiple venues, as in the case of Birmingham Museums and Art Gallery.

Manchester Art Gallery.

University: These are owned and run by a university. In addition to serving the needs of local communities, they aim to serve the needs of scholars and support research by university staff and students. If your university has a museum or gallery attached you might think about approaching them first. Examples include

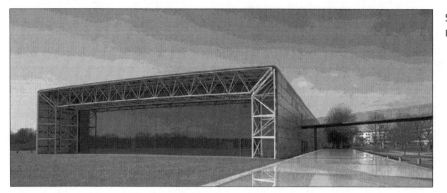

Sainsbury Centre for Visual Arts, University of East Anglia.

the Mead Gallery, University of Warwick, and the Sainsbury Centre for Visual Arts, University of East Anglia.

Independent: Independent Museums are those museums typically set up and run as charitable organisations. Over half of the 2,500 museums in the UK are independent. Examples include Abbot Hall, Kendal, the River and Rowing Museum, Henley on Thames, and Modern Art Oxford.

Many charities receive funding from a range of sources that combine local authorities and business sponsorship, as well as professional bodies such as the Arts Council England (ACE) that offer regular funding to arts organisations (known as Regularly Funded Organisations or RFOs) assigned to each Arts Council region.

Commercial/private galleries: These are primarily for the sale of artworks, though they may also host travelling exhibitions, for example the Rollo Art Gallery, London, and Fine Art Society, London.

National Trust/English Heritage: Buildings maintained and restored by these organisations are often good places to consider as exhibition venues.

How to Propose an Exhibition

The best approach is a personal one. Either look at the contact list on the museum website, or call the museum's general number and ask for the name of the curator, or the person responsible for organising the exhibition programme. Then, either arrange to have a telephone conversation or to meet up in person.

If you can, research the institution in advance, and ask to see a copy of their Exhibition Policy if they have one. It is important to note that forming a good relationship with staff is essential, and will improve the chances of your idea being accepted.

Most museums will require exhibition ideas in the form of a written proposal. The format of these varies from institution to institution but there are some aspects that will be required by all.

Exhibition proposals: some museum websites outline the procedure for proposing exhibitions, and have downloadable forms that you can fill in. Alternatively, you can request a form from the museum.

Subject: If possible, match your subject to the organisation. For example, if your exhibition discusses a particular group of artists, find an institution that has a

University museums
For a full list visit: www.umg.org.uk

Association of Independent Museums (AIMS)
www.aim-museums.co.uk

Example of proposal form
Birmingham Museums and Art Gallery Exhibitions Proposal Form, downloadable from:
www.bmag.org.uk/about/plans&policies

large number of their works in the collection. Many organisations have their collections online. If not, contact the relevant curator for this information.

Consider what exhibitions your chosen institution has put on in the past. Note that many museum and gallery websites include a list of past shows. Although they may be unwilling to put on an exhibition similar to a recent display, they may be interested in ideas that update successful shows put on 20 years or so ago.

Local authority museums are particularly keen on exhibitions about the area as they know they will bring in local people who are likely to make up the majority of their visitors.

Many organisations with multiple regular funders set different objectives for exhibitions' programming. For example, these galleries may offer a range of exhibition spaces, from an international high-profile gallery to a community space for local artists and/or outreach projects.

Timing: Museums like to have plenty of lead-in time to an exhibition. If the exhibition ties in with an anniversary, make sure you begin looking for an appropriate institution well in advance as there may be a lot of competition for exhibition slots.

The amount of time an institution will require will depend on the size of the exhibition and whether it will require any loans. The more international loans you envisage, the more years in advance you will need to put in a proposal. It is worth remembering that the costs of international loans can be very steep owing to travel and packing costs, and also the fact that many venues require **couriers** to accompany artworks.. For a major exhibition, a museum may want at least three to five years' notice. However, a smaller display or exhibition may only require six-months' notice.

> **Courier:** A representative from a lending institution who accompanies the artwork. A first-class ticket is frequently specified as part of the arrangement.

Scale of the exhibition: How many works will the exhibition involve? How many loans will it require? Will these be from the UK or from abroad (therefore more expensive)? When putting in a proposal it is best if you can give a rough idea of how many objects you will need, i.e. 20–30, 50–70, 160–180. This will give the institution a good idea of how much space will be required, and how much money they will need to finance it.

Try to see as many of your intended objects as possible. Do not assume that the objects you wish to view will be on display; telephone in advance of your visit, as you may need to make arrangements to visit stores or print rooms off-site. For contemporary art exhibitions, these trips may also include visits to artists' studios, and regular curatorial meetings with the artists regarding the development and display of their artworks. When you are there ask about whether they might consider lending the object, and whether it requires any conservation treatment.

Painting racks in the picture store at the Walker Art Gallery, National Museums Liverpool (© National Museums Liverpool).

Funding: In light of the current budget cuts, museums will be more interested in exhibitions that come with funding. Until the proposal is accepted, it would be almost impossible to guarantee funding, but adding an indication of potential funding opportunities to the proposal will make a stronger case. Would you expect to be paid a fee? If you are able to do it for the kudos alone this would be hugely beneficial to the museum's exhibition budget. A list of funders you could approach appears in the Appendix to this publication.

Tour: It is worth thinking early in the planning stages about venues to which the exhibition might travel. If there are going to be prohibitive costs (such as for conservation, crating the art works, or for a publication) then touring the exhibition is sometimes a possibility because these costs can then be split between all the venues.

Many funders, such as Arts Council England, may require up to three venues for their funding. Tours also increase the exhibition's exposure nationally and internationally. Increasingly, exhibitions are going to locations outside the USA and western Europe, including Turkey, Hungary, Russia, and China. The curator will often be invited to the tour venue to give a lecture on the subject of the show.

Palettised Artworks Ready for Shipment to the United States (© Heather Birchall).

What Happens Next?

Contract: A contract should be put in place as soon as possible between the academic and the museum or gallery. This will clarify the schedule (including dates of future meetings), fee (if applicable), and details regarding any publication. The contract should also set out various responsibilities, such as who will be writing the wall panels and labels.

Loans: Try to use as many objects as possible from the gallery's own collection. Loans, particularly international ones, are expensive, not only because of the cost of crating and transporting the object, and for the accompanying courier's ticket and accommodation, but because the Registrar of the lending institution will usually require a **facilities report** for every venue at which the loan will be exhibited. In any case, museums may prefer to promote their own collection rather than borrow works, especially during times of financial constraint.

Avoid fixating on one particular object from another institution that might be unavailable or require prohibitively expensive conservation treatment. If the exhibition does rely on the inclusion of a particular object, then check to see if it is available first before proceeding. Also, bear in mind that some works may be too vulnerable to travel. For example, works in chalk or pastel are extremely susceptible to damage from vibrations and, if requested for loan, are more likely to be turned down.

If an artwork you desire is in a private collection, it can be trickier to negotiate the loan. However, if the work has been included in a previous exhibition, then it is worth contacting that museum as they may still have the details of the owner, and may be willing to send a letter on your behalf. If a work has passed through an auction house in recent years then it is always worth getting in touch with the relevant auctioneer's department to ask them to forward a letter to the buyer.

As noted above, it is essential to see as many works as possible before requesting them for loan. This will allow you to assess their size (often quite different 'in the flesh') and the condition of both the work and its frame, if it has one. If it is not possible to see a work before requesting it, ask the gallery/collector for a high quality, up-to-date photograph instead.

When requesting items for loan, you may need to write paragraphs for the loan letters explaining why a particular work is crucial to the success of the exhibition (*see example right*).

Facilities report: The facilities report outlines an institution's facilities, climate, security, staffing, insurance, and loan history. Few institutions will agree to lend items without seeing the borrowing institutions' report. Samples of different types of facilities report can be accessed on UKRG (UK Registrars Group): www.ukregistrarsgroup.org/publications

Justification for the exhibition 'Blake's Shadow' held at the Whitworth Art Gallery, Manchester, in 2008

The exhibition will focus, in particular, on the way in which Blake's expression of the body as something at once decorative and physical allowed subsequent artists and designers to make the human form, rather than narrative, the central issue of pictorial composition. We have selected five works from your collection, as listed below, which would enable us to demonstrate this central theme:

N05058 William Blake *Newton*

N01647 G. F. Watts *Chaos*

T07734 Cecil Collins *The Poet*

T03836 John Craxton *Dreamer in a Landscape*

T07696 Keith Vaughan *Cain and Abel*

Newton, in particular, is absolutely crucial to the underlying argument as it highlights how the body-centred nature of Blake's large colour prints influenced Victorian and Neo-Romantic artists looking for a way of treating the body without using obvious narrative conventions.

Grouping: Once you have agreed on your list of objects, you can start thinking about groupings. In particular, decide which works should be hung adjacent, or in the same section. Also think about which objects you would like the visitor to see at the beginning and end of the show. At this point you might consider creating a scale model of the exhibition so you can make sure that everything fits in the gallery spaces. Spend as much time as you can in the proposed display spaces so you can get a feel for sight lines. Note that in larger organisations decisions about the final hang of the exhibition will rest with the director.

Exhibition catalogues/guides: In addition to text panels and labels within the exhibition you may also want to produce an exhibition catalogue or booklet. Whether you decide to produce a full-blown book or a smaller pamphlet may depend on the size of the collaborating organisation, their budget, and your ability to acquire funding. Also, consider whether you require funding for image copyrights as this may be beyond the means of the institution.

Although most major exhibitions are accompanied by a catalogue, it is best *not* to assume that your exhibition will be. Many museums are turning to online catalogues or smaller exhibition guides, which are far cheaper to produce and less of a financial risk. Some galleries, notably Tate, do have their own in-house publishers, but many work with a separate publisher to produce their catalogues.

Copyright: If the gallery does not have a picture researcher or picture librarian, it is likely that you will need to assist in obtaining copyright permission for any images to be used in the publication. Even if the organisation owns the work of art, it does not automatically mean that they hold the copyright, particularly if the artist is still alive or died within the last 70 years. If you are borrowing works from another institution, they often allow you to reproduce the work for free, but you must check before publishing. Do not assume that museums and galleries will be able to give discounts on images. Image reproduction is one of the most lucrative ways of bringing in revenue for these institutions, and you may need to budget quite a hefty amount to cover these costs.

Roles within Museums and Galleries

Each institution is different, but these are some of the personnel you may encounter. It is worth noting that in smaller organisations one person may fill a number of the roles.

Curator: It is most likely that you will be working closely with one of the gallery's own curators to create the exhibition. This will probably be someone who shares your specialisation, but in smaller museums, where there may be just one curator, your partnership may be based on your knowledge of a particular subject and their experience in curating exhibitions. Your museum-based co-curator may well take care of the more logistical side of preparations, but you may be required to help write loan letters and produce interpretation such as text panels and labels. The gallery curator is likely to hang the exhibition, but may want you to be on hand to offer opinions. However, each partnership will be different and it is a good idea to say near the start of the project what you feel comfortable doing or are keen to be involved in.

Press officer: The press team are there to drum up interest in your exhibition. They will need as much information as you can give them, as early as you can give it, to write a press release. Some releases will go out months in advance, and these will then be followed up nearer the start of the exhibition. Press releases are likely to go out to newspapers, magazines, radio stations, TV channels, websites, and societies who might be interested in the exhibition. The press officer is likely to arrange a press call that will involve members of the media viewing the exhibition and talking to the curators. They may also set up separate interviews for radio or television. If you can think of magazines or groups who may be interested in your exhibition, let the press officer know. Build a good relationship with the press officer and take time to explain the exhibition to them so that they know exactly what to promote. Ask to see a copy of the press release before it goes out in case facts have got altered along the way.

Press releases
Examples can be found at:
www.tate.org.uk/about/pressoffice/
pressreleases

Marketing officer: The press and marketing officer may be the same person, but in bigger organisations the marketing team tend to be separate from the press team. Marketing's job is to get people through the door and into your exhibition. As with press officers, the more you can tell them in advance the better. They will organise advertising in magazines, newspapers, on trains etc, but are also likely to be responsible for exhibition signage outside the gallery (for example on banners). They may want to decide on the exhibition title, and choose a lead image. The latter is often based on several possible images you have sent them. Do not be too disheartened if they do not go for the one you think will work best. Their job is to know what is enticing for the public; this may be different from the object that the curator finds most exciting! Marketing work closely with designers to create content for posters, banners, leaflets, and email shots. Bear in mind that printing is often done well in advance, so give marketing as much notice as possible of the opening date of the exhibition, and have images ready well in advance to give to them. Make sure that you have cleared the copyright for any images you give to marketing.

Web/social media officer: The web officer runs the museum's website, and often other related social media, such as those on Facebook, Twitter, and MySpace. They may also write a blog about the museum and want to visit during installation to take shots that might interest the public, who rarely get to see behind the scenes. If you are giving a talk, they may also want to record it so that it can be broadcast online or as a podcast.

Exhibition officer: In larger organisations there is an exhibition team as well as a curatorial team. Whereas curators research and create the hang of a show, the exhibition officer looks after the logistics of putting it on. They liaise with the handling team, designers, joiners (who often make the cabinets, and false walls), painters, electricians etc. They create a schedule for the hang and de-installation, and often organise project team meetings attended by all those involved in getting the exhibition up, often also including staff from learning, conservation, marketing, and press. When installing the display, the exhibition officer will be on hand to make sure that the installation runs smoothly. In smaller organisations, where this role does not exist, it may well fall to the museum curator to project manage the exhibition.

Registrar: The registrar is responsible for requesting and organising all matters relating to the loan of artworks you may require from other organisations. The curator may wish to send out the initial loan request, or liaise closely with the registrar in the first instance. Once a loan is agreed, the registrar looks after the paperwork associated with it. They complete loan forms, send back any environmental **condition reports** required by the loan organisation, and organise transport to collect the work. They will also arrange for insurance under the **Government Indemnity Scheme**, and the per diem, accommodation, and additional transport for couriers accompanying any loan objects.

Technicians/handling team: The technicians are responsible for unpacking the works, and physically installing the exhibition. They work to a plan set out by the curators and/or the designers. If the objects are going into display cases, a curator or conservator may prefer to do the actual installation.

Conservators: Conservators often oversee the installation of works in the exhibition. If the objects are from the art gallery's own collection, they are likely to have inspected them at an early stage in case any remedial work needs to be done before they can be displayed. When loans are involved, the relevant conservator (painting, sculpture, ceramics, textile) will be there when the crate is opened. Most objects arrive with a conservation report filled in by the loan organisation. The host conservator will study this and complete their own report, recording and reporting any damage that has occurred during transport. This is done before the object is installed. The conservator will also complete a report when the object is de-installed to check that no damage has occurred whilst the object has been in the exhibition.

Designers: In smaller organisations, the layout of the exhibition may be created by the curator, but in bigger art galleries and museums there is often a separate design department. They design leaflets, banners, and other marketing material, but are often heavily involved in the hang of the exhibition too. They are likely to design the layout of the exhibition based on the sections and groupings provided by the curator. This may involve the use of false walls and cases, and the design of additional structures, should they be needed. The designers may even build a small model. Once the curator has written the text, the designers create the labels, wall panels, and any additional graphics, and organise for them to be printed.

Learning team: There may be several roles within the learning team. One officer is likely to be responsible for working with schools and organising school visits. There may also be an officer who focuses solely on putting together a programme of educational events such as curator talks, lectures, family workshops, and concerts as part of the exhibition. Some learning teams may also have a community or outreach officer who will arrange visits from various community groups, and could also facilitate community collaboration in the exhibition if suitable. It is good to work with the learning team as soon as possible so that they can plan their events around the exhibition and generate publicity. Their advertising may be printed well in advance, so it is worth making sure they are present at project team meetings.

Gallery manager and visitor services assistants: The gallery manager looks after the day-to-day running of the gallery. They manage the front-of-house staff, and also ensure that the building is safe, clean, and secure. You may want to do a staff briefing before the exhibition opens to the public. This will allow you to talk the front of house staff through the exhibition, and give you the chance to point out any particularly vulnerable works that may require extra security.

Condition report: A report completed by the conservator which records the condition of the art work, generally before and after it has been transported to another institution in case any damage occurs whilst it is travelling to, or being installed in, the exhibition.

Government Indemnity Scheme: This provides borrowing institutions with an alternative to the cost of commercial insurance. For example, a museum, gallery or library can borrow objects from non-national institutions and, in the event of loss or damage, compensation will be paid to the owner by the government. Applying for GIS is often the only way smaller museums can afford to stage large exhibitions with multiple loans.

Text checking
You may be required, and it is always good practice, to make sure that someone in the education team reads any text to go into the exhibition in order to make sure it is clear and accessible.

Installing the Exhibition

Preparation: Several months before the installation of the exhibition it is likely that a project team meeting will be held to discuss dates, budgets, loans, marketing, press, and events. As the exhibition gets nearer, there may be further project team meetings held so that everyone knows what is expected of them. An installation schedule should be drawn up showing the installation period day by day, and detailing exactly what is happening and when. Although this may change, and things may have to be re-scheduled during the installation, it is useful to have a timetable to work with, especially if it is a large exhibition with a number of teams involved.

Exhibition space: Well in advance, a number of things need to be considered. What colours should the walls be painted? Will there be enough plug sockets for the required display cases, and are they in convenient places? Electronic and new-media artworks failing a PAT (Portable Appliance Testing) test may need to be withdrawn from an exhibition. Find out whether new-media work is appropriately tested for health and safety prior to the installation. Is there enough time for paint fumes to off-gas so that they do not damage works of art? Will there be adequate security to sit with works that have not yet been hung whilst the handling team go for lunch/tea break? Small things such as these are not obvious, but can cause last-minute panic to the exhibition team. Although these may well be taken care of by the collaborating curator, it is important to consider these kinds of details.

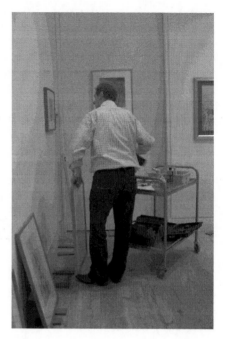

Technician Tony Rae hanging artworks for exhibition Whitechapel at War: Isaac Rosenberg and his Circle at the Stanley & Audrey Burton Gallery, University of Leeds, 2008 (© Layla Bloom).

Installing loans: If you are borrowing objects from other institutions or individuals, they will require a great deal of preparation and installation time. Transport and insurance needs to be organised in advance and, when it comes to installing the exhibition, it is likely that most objects will come with an accompanying courier from the institution that owns the work(s). The courier's role is to oversee the unpacking of the object and its installation. If the object is a painting or a work on paper, most organisations will require the host institution to place the travelling container or crate in the room in which they are to be hung for 24 or 48 hours before they can be unpacked, to allow the work time to acclimatise. The courier will also want to watch the installation of the object and may require additional security measures (alarms, barriers) to be put in place if they feel the work is particularly vulnerable.

Hanging paintings and works on paper: There are a number of methods for hanging pictures or framed works on paper, and each institution may have slight variations.

If the organisation has a design team, they will have created a hang based on information supplied by yourself and the curator about the size of the pictures and your groupings. Creating the hang may take several meetings, and may result in compromises having to be made with the designer. Often, curators are keen to fit in as much as possible, and the designer may be the one to show them that realistically not every item can fit in.

When hanging the exhibition it is likely that the hang may have to deviate from the design plan. This is often because, in practice, two works that looked great together on paper clash terribly in real life. It is up to the curator to get the balance of artworks right, and this may mean having to rethink a hang on the

Gallery team installing exhibition Aspects of British Printmaking c. 1860–1980 at the Stanley & Audrey Burton Gallery, University of Leeds, 2008 (© Layla Bloom).

spot. If this happens, asking the handling team to try out potential hangs by propping the works up where you would like them to go can help you to create a solution.

Whichever type of hanging style you are using, spacing needs to be worked out beforehand. This may need to include leaving space for labels. It is often helpful to ask the handling team to prop up the pictures in the position in which they will be hung to check spacing before they drill into the wall. Often the handling team uses a **bradawl** to make the initial holes before drilling into the wall.

Methods for attaching objects to walls:

Rods: A bar is secured to the top of the wall. This will need to be weight-tested beforehand to ensure that it is strong enough to hold the artwork. Hooks are then secured to the back of the frame by the handlers. When hanging loaned works, the courier will need to give permission for new hooks to be added to the frame, and care must be taken that new holes are not drilled too close to existing ones in case they split the frame.

Two hooked rods are attached to the bar. These hang down but may need to be moved once the painting is hung in case they are leaning in or have splayed out. Security hooks are slid onto the rods. These hooks only move when no weight is resting on them. Loose rings are attached to these hooks. When the handlers hang the painting they will hook these rings over the hooks on the back of the painting. Using the security hooks, and carefully lifting one side of the painting at a time, the artwork can be straightened. Most galleries have an in-house hanging height to which you may need to adhere.

This method is useful where it is impossible to drill into the wall (e.g. when the walls are not painted but covered in fabric which would easily show up marks from repeated re-hanging). It also allows the freedom to take a work off the wall or move paintings around if any works need rearranging.

Allow for corners
If hanging close to a corner, extra space may need to be given on the side closest to the corner to avoid the picture looking squashed.

Bradawl: a pointed boring tool used to mark the position for a hole to be drilled.

Rods being used to hang a picture.

Chains: These are a variation of hanging on rods and the method is very similar. The disadvantage of hanging with chains is that they can get twisted. However, in historic buildings they can look extremely good, and in keeping with the décor of the building, unlike more modern-looking rods.

Mirror plates and screws: This is the most common method of hanging pictures. The painting is turned over and three mirror plates attached. A safety or security screw, requiring a unique type of screwdriver to undo it, is often used for additional security. Heavier paintings may need to rest on brackets, which add extra support. These are screwed into the wall and levelled using a spirit level. Before making holes in the wall, the handling team will work out the spacing between works and the height at which to hang the picture, using a measuring tape and a spirit level

Most organisations have a set **hanging height**, which fits with access standards. However, if your exhibition is aimed at children you may want to think about having a lower hanging height, or ways of making the works more accessible to children.

Display cases: There are numerous types of display cases. Some only require a set of keys to open; others may need the handling team to open the case using glass suckers. Find out well in advance how to open your chosen display cases as you may require support from the handling team. If installing ceramic or textile pieces, you may want to enlist the help of the relevant conservator. You may also need additional support for delicate items such as cloth garments, on which a conservator can advise. If the organisation has a design team, they are likely to have created a display case layout based on information provided by you about the sizes and groupings of objects. Remember to include any bases and stands in these measurements. You should include any requests for additional stands or mirrors to highlight certain objects.

Sculptures: These often require greater preparation to display as they may need plinths to be built to hold them; floors may have to be weight-tested in advance if the sculpture is particularly heavy. Deciding on how to display the work may require liaising with a sculpture conservator who will know which works would be at greater risk if put on open display. Smaller sculptures may need to go in a display case for security reasons. Some works may need additional support to secure them to a plinth if they are likely to topple, or if they have an uneven base. Silicon can often be a simple solution to this, but a conservator must approve any support in case it damages the work.

Security: If you are hoping to have works on open display or to allow visitors to interact with/walk around installation works, you need you find out well in advance how visitor assistants/museum security will patrol the exhibition area. Often, for budget reasons, visitor assistants may work on a roving patrol system, and it may not be possible to have a member of security staff continually next to a work. If this is the case, you will need to work out with the designer how to display a vulnerable work. It may require creating a smaller room within a large exhibition space using temporary walls known as **panelock screens**, or using barriers to prevent visitors from getting too close to an artwork.

Small works and display cases often have individual alarms. These may be linked directly to the control room, and the gallery manager will need to know in

Chains used for hanging *Portrait of Fanny, Lady Fildes* (© National Museums Liverpool).

Standard mirror-plate (© National Museums Liverpool).

T-bar mirror-plate (© National Museums Liverpool).

Hanging height: The preferred measurement from the floor to the centre of the work. Unless the work is very large, the average hanging height is 62 inches/158 cm. Hanging a work too high, or out of view, is known as 'skying'.

Panelock screens: These can be used to create temporary walls (© Heather Birchall).

advance before a work is moved so that they are not panicked when an alarm is triggered. Allow enough time to add new alarms if needed, as each one is likely to have a unique code that has to be installed.

The position of security cameras and alarms should be considered, especially if a painting is unglazed or on open display. More vulnerable works like these may need barriers around them to prevent visitors from getting too close.

Lighting: The level of lighting will depend on the items you have on display. Works on paper and textiles require far lower lighting levels; the level should be at about 50 lux. Paintings should be lit at about 150 lux.

If at all possible it is best practice to have a conservator with you as you adjust the lighting levels, particularly if you are including loan works in the display.

In some organisations the lighting is altered by electricians, who may need to be booked in advance. In others it may be the design team who alter the levels remotely using a computer system. Lighting systems tracks vary, and may not be as flexible as you had hoped. Finding out in advance how easy it is to dim the lights in a particular area may affect your layout.

And finally... A day or two before the show opens, the curator will be responsible for 'snagging' – looking for any defects or things that need attention.

Interpretation

Interpretation refers to the text panels, labels, any other graphics such as vinyls, and also interactive devices such as touch screens or smartphones, which are used in an exhibition. It is highly likely that you would be involved in writing some of the text. Some galleries have an in-house style and way of writing. For example, Manchester Art Gallery uses the Ekarv System, which generally employs simple language, and reflects the natural rhythm of speech.

Increasingly. museums are making the most of digital media, and **QR codes** are being positioned next to physical objects, to enable visitors to access further information.

Most institutions specify a word limit far shorter than you might expect. Anywhere between 50 and 150 words is usual for a label, 150 to 200 for a text panel. Labels will need key information such as title, date, artist, medium, and accession number. They should also include a credit line, which describes how the object entered the collection, e.g. 'Presented by Miss Theresa Green in 1883', or the name of the loan institution. These details are often referred to as the 'tombstone', and galleries are likely to have a set way of arranging this information.

If you are required to write interpretation, ask to see previous labels and text panels to get a feel for how the gallery likes information to be presented. University galleries may require a more academic style of writing, whilst a local authority museum may want you to use a more accessible style, with shorter sentences and fewer words. If you are co-curating the show, divide up the text between the curators, write it and then read each other's before editing.

Some galleries may use their design department to create the labels. Designers usually like to receive the text well in advance – often as long as six months for a

Ekarv System: An approach to composing labels in a format accessible to the non-specialist. It includes using simple sentences, short lines of text, and organising the information in a way that will seem logical to the non-specialist. For an example, see: www.museums.4t.com/Articles/ Article33.htm

QR code: A two-dimensional bar-code, placed near to the object, or on the label. It can be scanned into a mobile phone (with the appropriate software or app), taking the user to a website carrying additional information.

Artist Andrew Warstat creating a site-specific artwork for the exhibition 'The Object of Photography' at the Stanley & Audrey Burton Gallery, University of Leeds, 2009 (© Layla Bloom).

major project, or two months for a small display. Find out how long the team will need and factor this in. Once you have written your text it may well need to be seen by a number of people, such as the education team and the gallery director, which will take extra time. Smaller galleries may not use a designer; the labels may be made by the curator, and text panels may be sent out to a local printer. If this is the case, find out in advance the dimensions of the label holders, as this may establish your word limit. Text panels and graphics can eat into budgets, so think well in advance how many will be needed.

Once everyone is happy with the text, it will need proofreading. Try to give yourself some time away from what you have written so that you can come to it with fresh eyes. Don't just read it on screen. Print it out. And find someone not involved in the project to check it as well. They will notice far more mistakes than you will.

Exhibition Opening and Events

Exhibition opening: The press office will collate a guest list for the opening, to which you may wish to have an input, and will sometimes seek sponsorship for the refreshments. The museum/gallery may wish to invite a special guest to open the exhibition and give a speech.

Events: Increasingly, events such as academic conferences, informal study days looking at a particular artistic movement or techniques, and curator-led talks for the public are organised to coincide with exhibitions. These generally need to be planned well in advance.

Font size
Remember that galleries need to use at least 18pt text to comply with access standards on their labels.

Deinstallation and Evaluation

Deinstallation: Inevitably, the show has to end, and the walls have to be cleared and repainted for the next exhibition It is always quicker to take down (strike) an exhibition than to install one. You may have to make provision for couriers returning to oversee deinstallation of works, and for booking specialist teams if any building, technical, or lighting effects created especially for the exhibition have to be dismantled.

In addition, loaned works will have to be re-packaged and re-crated ready for transportation.

Evaluation: Visitors' comments books can often provide a useful source of feedback relating to an exhibition. In addition, museums and galleries often have an evaluation meeting after the exhibition has closed. The following may be considered:

♦ Were the expectations of the visitors met?

♦ How has the exhibition increased and diversified audiences?

♦ In what ways has the exhibition made an intellectual and cultural contribution?

♦ How did visitors respond to the interpretation?

Evaluations: Thorough exhibition evaluations can be found on the Natural History Museum site: www.nhm.ac.uk/about-us/visitor-research/exhibitions/index.html

Packing: The main three ways in which objects are wrapped for transport are via crates, travelling frames (t-frames), and softwrapping.

Crates (*see below*) are fully enclosed boxes and are standard for international loans. They provide the greatest protection for an object, but are expensive.

Travelling frames (*see below*) are boxes open at one side; the object is secured within it using mirror-plates and the entire t-frame is then wrapped in polythene. They are often used for loans travelling short distances, and are lighter and cheaper than crates. However, they do not provide the same level of protection. (Image © Heather Birchall)

Softwrapping is wrapping an object directly using bubble-wrap, acid-free tissue, foam-wrap or polythene. This is suitable only for short journeys as the object can be vulnerable.

Presenting Contemporary Art
in Regional Art Galleries and Centres

Dr Outi Remes

Head of Exhibitions, South Hill Park Arts Centre, Bracknell (2007–11)

Many regional art galleries and centres offer curated programmes and a good variety of exhibition space and support. In 2007, I took up post as Head of Exhibitions at South Hill Park Arts Centre in Bracknell, Berkshire, following my PhD in History of Art at the University of Reading, and six years of freelance lecturing and curatorial work.

South Hill Park is the largest arts centre in Berkshire, and receives 250,000 visitors annually. Besides music, dance, digital media, theatre, and workshop programmes, South Hill Park organises over 20 annual exhibitions of contemporary art in purpose-built gallery and exhibition areas in the Centre's Grade II listed 18th-century mansion and gardens. In addition to visual arts shows, the exhibitions department presents interactive and new media work such as sound and live art.

Most shows are curated by the Centre's staff, but we also invite visiting curators to work on projects, and have open calls on specific subjects such as sound and live art. We also receive one or two touring shows from other galleries every year. The mansion space exhibitions are often thematic and based on the main show in the Centre's white cube space, the Bracknell Gallery, in the new part of the building. The Bracknell Gallery exhibitions are programmed 18 to 24 months before the exhibition opens. We welcome proposals from academics, galleries, artists, and artist groups. Informal introductions from our current or previous partners or other publicly funded galleries are often useful. While we consider all unsolicited material, we only accept a small number of the proposals, mostly for the Community Gallery.

We have worked with several academics on exhibition projects. South Hill Park recently worked with the University of Reading on a group architecture exhibition, Architectural Fictions, curated by Mary Maclean and Tim Renshaw (2010). Other recent exhibitions by academics have included Virtually Sculpture (2009) by Michael Shaw (*see right*). The exhibition followed his three-year AHRC fellowship at Loughborough University, exploring the sculptural potential of computer-aided design and manufacture to extend Donald Judd's concept of Specific Objects (1965). Also in 2009, we worked with Michael Takeo Magruder (King's College, London) on his Addressable Memory multimedia exhibition that considered the critical and aesthetic notions of 'memory' within contemporary life in our information-dependent society.

The exhibition's programme includes related projects, and events such as symposia, talks, and publications. For example, the Conspiracy Dwellings exhibition (2007–08), presenting work by Pam Skelton (Central Saint Martins College of Art & Design) with contributions by C. CRED, Tina Clausmeyer, and

Installation of Michael Shaw's *INF6* (2008, PVC, air, 240x160x90) for Virtually Sculpture exhibition, South Hill Park, 2009 (© Areej Abdi).

Verena Kyselka, represented a study of the topography of surveillance in a former East German city from the perspective of the 'conspiracy dwellings' designated by the Stasi as venues to meet with their unofficial informers. The exhibition included an international symposium, co-organised by South Hill Park and Pam Skelton, with both invited speakers and an open call. The symposium was funded by Arts Council England, Artist Resource Centre, and AHRC and was followed by the collection, *Conspiracy Dwellings: Surveillance in Contemporary Art* (Cambridge Scholars Publishing, 2010), edited by myself and Pam Skelton.

While many exhibition proposals represent interesting artwork, we consider the proposals in relation to a number of criteria, in particular the quality of ideas and how they relate to the gallery's remit. A successful exhibition encourages conversation, and communicates with our audience, allowing space for further thinking. Representing recently created artwork is rewarding as, by bringing the artwork from the studio to public domain, opportunities are presented to discuss the artist's work.

Moreover, a successful proposal must fit with the mission of the exhibition space. Many organisations include a note about their objectives and a mission statement on their websites. Many galleries also engage with major regional and national events such as the 2012 Olympics. South Hill Park's season programming varies from a local focus to showcasing international artists who challenge definitions of art. The programming often combines multiple art forms across the departments. Furthermore, different exhibition spaces in the Centre have specific profiles, and opportunities for showing installations differ; some are invigilated and allow complex installations, while other spaces may require a site-specific commission due to being an access space in a Grade II listed hall. If a venue has multiple galleries, academics should investigate, as far as possible, the requirements and purpose of each space. Visiting a venue before putting in a proposal is therefore essential.

Hints on Drawing up a Proposal

When submitting a proposal you should present it in a form that is easily accessible to the selection panel. From the outset it is important to be clear about the budget, technical requirements, and timetable of your exhibition. It is helpful to know whether the work(s) has been exhibited previously or is touring to other venues. Moreover, you should specify if you require any unusual equipment for the exhibition – for example, if the piece requires a smoke machine to create particular effects, you should check in advance that the gallery has one, and that it can be booked out for your use for the duration of the show. As South Hill Park has two theatres and a music bar, we receive requests for audio and lighting equipment we stock but cannot book out for several weeks due to their shared use. Also, if, for example, you require several projectors, many curators will be delighted if you mention that you can source some of them independently. South Hill Park provides marketing support and organises press releases, a seasonal brochure, exhibitions leaflet, and online listings. However, if you wish to have a full page in *Frieze* magazine for example, many galleries have such a budget for a few exhibitions only, so this is where additional funding helps.

South Hill Park, like many publicly funded art centres and galleries, is a charity, and operates with tight resources. Our focus on contemporary art enables us to

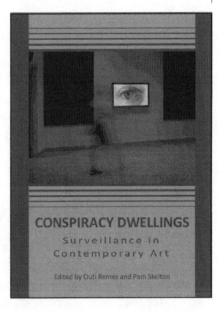

Cover of book based on symposium held at South Hill Park Arts Centre, 2010.

Mary Oliver, The University of Salford, work-in-progress during the public access hours in the Bracknell Gallery, *Rules and Regs* live art residencies, South Hill Park, 2009 (© Nancy Millner).

work with artists as closely as possible prior to the exhibition, but the art centre has limited administrative resources. Also, owing to the high number of annual projects, it is not possible to work on multiple funding applications for every exhibition. We offer in-kind support and match funding (a part contribution that other funding bodies may match). We encourage visiting curators and artists to look for further funding independently. There are several funding bodies, such as Grants for the Arts (The Arts Council), The Esmée Fairbairn Foundation, Paul Hamlyn Foundation, The Elephant Trust, The Wellcome Trust, Arts and Business, and The Foundation for Sport and the Arts, to name a few (*see also the list in the Appendix*). Some funders prioritise exhibitions that have secured more than one venue, although the venues should not share the immediate audience catchment area. It is also worth contacting a local council and considering business sponsorship that may come in the form of equipment and materials.

In summary, when proposing an exhibition make sure you:

♦ Know your venue, its audience, its exhibition policy, spaces, and objectives.

♦ Make it clear why you have chosen this curator/venue.

♦ Explain how its audience will benefit from the exhibition.

♦ Show that you have considered practicalities such as the timetable, funding, transport, equipment, administration, and marketing.

♦ Clearly state any technical requirements.

Curating 'Roman to English'
A Collaborative Experience

Professor Catherine Karkov

University of Leeds

The sculpture of Roman Britain and Anglo-Saxon England has traditionally been approached from an archaeological viewpoint concerned with establishing the style, subject matter, and historical context of objects rather than with understanding them as works of art. Centred upon the four faces of the supporting shaft of a tall free-standing stone cross, the objects in Roman to English: The Migration of Forms in Early Northumberland were grouped together in such a way as to suggest that we look at them not as artefacts but as works of art that not only speak to each other, but are also active participants in larger discourses of political, national, and cultural identity.

Roman to English was a small exhibition, held in Gallery 4 at the Henry Moore Institute in Leeds from 10 July to 10 October 2010. It grew out of an invitation from Penelope Curtis, then curator of the Henry Moore Institute, to work with the Institute on developing an exhibition of Anglo-Saxon stone sculpture. Nothing was definite. The exhibition was only a possibility. With colleagues from the University of Leeds, I made a formal presentation to the Institute and suggested a theme dealing with the transition from Romano-Britain to Anglo-Saxon England, and using sculpture from along the line of Hadrian's Wall. That proposal was accepted and we began to explore two different scenarios. The first was a major exhibition in the Institute's main galleries that would require external funding; the second was a much more limited exhibition in the small gallery that could be funded from within the HMI's annual budget. We ended up opting for the latter for several reasons: it was much easier to accomplish, it wouldn't rely on research council funding applications which no one involved really had the time to write and, perhaps most importantly, the sculpture itself is not always easy to procure or exhibit.

Selecting the Sculptures

Our next step was to sift through hundreds of images of sculpture, some of it still *in situ*, and other pieces housed in various museums and church collections from across the north of England. This was very much a joint effort. Penelope, curatorial assistant Ellen Tait, and I viewed all the images together, sorted them into groups of sub-themes, debated their importance, the problems they presented, and so forth. We narrowed our selection down to sculptures that fitted into four stylistic or iconographic sub-themes. And together we spent a day travelling around the area of Hadrian's Wall to view as many of the sculptures as possible. Some of them turned out to be much too big to fit in the gallery space, or much too difficult to transport from their current location inside a remote church. Others were deemed to lack the style, clarity, or pure visual interest that would appeal to a general audience, even if they did have immense theoretical importance to me as an academic. The two sculptures that I felt were most essential to the exhibition were a Roman altar re-carved in Anglo-Saxon times, and a sculpture of a Victory figure from the old Roman fort of Stanwix in Cumbria. However, the first was too big, too worn, not visually appealing, and would have had to have been transported across a muddy farm field by tractor. The second was simply too big and too heavy, and by this point we had eliminated most of the other works with which it would have resonated (although I still want to do an exhibition around it).

Making Plans

In the end we settled on five sculptures, and from that point on Ellen and I did almost all of the planning of the exhibition together. We decided on placement of the sculptures – though really as one was a sculpture in the round (a cross-shaft), and the other four relief sculptures, the layout of the exhibition was dictated by the works themselves. The cross-shaft would sit in the centre of the room with the other pieces placed against each of the surrounding four walls. This made the visual connections between the works clear, and allowed viewers enough room to stand back from the works. It also had the added benefit of inscribing a cross in the space of the gallery, an interesting way of suggesting the appropriation of the old Roman world by the new Christian one. Together, we decided on the colour of the walls, and the design and content of the exhibition leaflet. I wrote a draft of the leaflet, sent it to Ellen for her input and criticism, and we wrote back and forth in this way until we both had the text we wanted.

Communication is Key

All in all, working with the Henry Moore Institute was a thoroughly enjoyable experience and a genuine collaboration. I may have disagreed initially with Penelope when she felt that some of the works I wanted in the exhibition were, well, not exactly sculpture, but she was quite right. From an academic perspective they might have been fascinating, and embodied everything I wanted the exhibition to communicate, but if the viewer needed to know the whole of their (often obscure) history in order to understand them, then they were in fact completely incapable of communicating the things I wanted them to say. I may have come up with the theme for the exhibition, but it was only in our planning meetings when Ellen, Penelope, and I viewed, debated and discussed the works together that the possibilities and nuances of the theme began to take shape. The exhibition proved to me that research and curating have to be done side by side. All projects and all collaborations are different, and it therefore goes without saying that there are things that Ellen or I would do differently in future, but they would be things that developed naturally out of the subject and goals of the project rather than things that arose in the course of our collaboration on this particular exhibition.

Heavenfield, near Hadrian's Wall, Northumberland (© Catherine Karkov).

An Art Historian as Guest Curator

A personal view

Dr Colin Cruise

The School of Art, Aberystwyth University

The most exciting way in which I have been able to present my research ideas in recent years has been through exhibitions. They have provided me with new opportunities to present my work in more accessible ways than academic publishing or teaching has done. It is work that has required me to re-think my skills and acquire new ones, and the process has been very rewarding.

The mixture of types of information and visual stimulation offered by exhibitions is immediately engaging. Behind the screens and information boards, the artful groupings of works of art and supporting evidence, lies a huge investment of time and effort. Time, indeed, is very much of the essence: the research has to be fairly complete before the gallery or museum is approached, the bids for funding and sponsorship have to be made before most of the other tasks are undertaken. Above all, in the midst of many other demanding processes, the catalogue has to be compiled, illustrated, edited, proofread, and designed.

Luckily, on the two occasions that I have curated big, touring exhibitions – both for Birmingham Museum and Art Gallery (BMAG) – I have been assigned an in-house curator, Victoria Osborne, who has been my chief contact with the museum's committees, administrators, and specialist departments. Victoria has liaised on my behalf – or, more correctly, on behalf of the project – with, among other departments, conservation, interpretation, publicity, and the registrar's office. She has been closely involved with all stages of both projects. As 'guest curator', as my role is described, I have found myself part of a team of professionals who have as much commitment to the realisation of the project as I have myself. The guest curator gets to do the rewarding and creative jobs, such as choosing the works, constructing narratives and themes, and designing the 'hang', while, behind the scenes, the museum team is having to undertake less glamorous, if essential, jobs, such as fundraising, sponsorship, insurance, and transportation.

Before I acted as guest curator for large international exhibitions I organised a few small exhibitions in studio spaces and university art galleries. These were important in introducing me to the various developmental stages in exhibition organisation, and I gained much from them. Sometimes, however, I had to learn important lessons through bitter experience.

An early melancholy history

Despite the humble nature of my earliest exhibitions, I felt equipped – mistakenly, as it turned out – to tackle more ambitious curatorial projects. The first of these was particularly unhappy, but it helped highlight the things that can go wrong. It began by my being approached by a small gallery with some reputation to work on an exhibition on a subject dear to my heart and on which I had done much original research. I suggested the exhibition's theme and organised it into sections but, as it moved towards its final form, the in-house curator insisted upon naming herself as sole curator. As a result, my authorship of the original research material was not acknowledged. I was thanked in the catalogue, although no more fulsomely than any of the other people on the list of acknowledgements. I had no contract and there was nothing I could do to prevent this lack of acknowledgement of my work. Walking out at a late stage seemed counterproductive, probably resulting in no credit at all. It is clear that I should have asked for a written agreement at the start of the project to ensure that my work was credited properly and my interests as a researcher protected.

My more recent experiences as guest curator for the two exhibitions at Birmingham Museum and Art Gallery have been hugely rewarding, and on that fruitful connection I have based my subsequent observations. I have learned what constitutes good practices by working in a thoroughly professional setting. It is significant that, in the initial stages of collaboration, BMAG were keen to set out not only what duties they expected the guest curator to undertake, but also what their responsibilities were towards me. Our responsibilities to each other were set out in properly drawn-up contracts.

Towards the Exhibition

Although the product of much effort, the exhibition installation is only the final stage of several developmental processes. Before the works are hung on the walls, the labels attached, and the information boards put in place, all the other processes have to have been successfully completed. From the proposal and the loan requests, the funding applications and the publishing contracts, the condition reports and the technical briefings – all need to be complete before the exhibition opening. I stress the importance of these processes because they are often overlooked and, although they are invisible to the visitor, are what preoccupy the curatorial team for months or years.

Love Revealed installation view, Gas Hall, Birmingham Museum & Art Gallery (© Birmingham Museums & Art Gallery).

Love Revealed' was held at BMAG in the autumn/winter of 2005, and travelled to the Villa Stuck in Munich in the spring of 2006 and to the Ben-Uri Gallery, the London Jewish Museum of Art, in the summer of that year. The catalogue was published by Merrell.

Both my BMAG exhibitions, Love Revealed: Simeon Solomon and the Pre-Raphaelites, and The Poetry of Drawing: Pre-Raphaelite Designs, Studies and Watercolours, began with my presentation of a proposal that outlined a working title and indicated the main themes of the exhibition, its aims and audiences. For the first, I was approached by the museum to curate an exhibition that would use their collection of works by Solomon and his contemporaries to best advantage. Nevertheless, although they approached me, I had to write a proposal that outlined how I would approach such an exhibition – its sections, the featured works, proposed loans: the 'story' of the exhibition, in other words, and its rationale. For the second example I approached the museum with an idea that would make best use of their vast holdings of Pre-Raphaelite drawings, most of which had rarely been seen by the public (the match between the proposal and the host institution is of great importance in making your 'pitch', needless to stay). Again, a proposal had to be written and, as in the first example, had to be considered by the museum's Exhibition Committee in a process consisting of several stages of close scrutiny of the documentation I had produced. I was not called upon to defend it in a presentation or interview, so all my ideas had to be in place within the proposal documentation, and made available to its readers.

In my experience, the proposal document should be as clear, concise, and focused as possible, concentrating upon the exact nature of the project and the intended impact on both scholarly and general audiences. An important aspect of this stage is to outline key works that are desirable for inclusion, with selected images. The proposal should make clear the importance, even uniqueness, of your exhibition, explaining why it is worth considering.

The decision-making process might take some time. The feasibility of exhibition proposals is tested by committees, and examined closely in various ways, not least for financial viability. It may be that your proposal would prove too expensive, might be too scholarly or have too narrow a focus. You may well have to answer further questions about possible external funding or sponsorship. If accepted, the project has to proceed, gradually and efficiently, in clear stages, some of which I list above. All these stages will bring you into contact with teams of other professionals who will want clear ideas from you.

Publications

Exhibitions can have a variety of publishing outcomes – a guide or hand-list, a catalogue or a book; each of them having different expectations about the nature of the text, the number of illustrations, and the word-length. If the guest curator is contracted to write a text, the museum or gallery will still be involved with the publication processes. They will take an active role in its production, through the provision of illustrations, negotiations with copyright holders and other editorial matters.

While a catalogue might seem the obvious outcome, a publisher who takes the project on might want to specify that the publication should be a book with a potentially longer shelf life and a wider audience than those who have visited the exhibition during its fixed dates. In all events, images are bound to be an issue. Even if you have the right to publish an image of a work that you intend to borrow for the exhibition, you might still need to acquire (and most probably purchase) images of alternative versions, studies, or related works to illustrate

Poetry of Drawing installation view, Gas Hall, Birmingham Museum & Art Gallery (© Birmingham Museums & Art Gallery).

The exhibition The Poetry of Drawing: Pre-Raphaelite Designs, Studies and Watercolours opened at BMAG in January 2011 and toured to the Gallery of New South Wales, Sydney, where it opened in June 2011.

A book accompanying the exhibition, Pre-Raphaelite Drawing, is published by Thames and Hudson.

alongside it for comparative purposes. This becomes a budgetary issue, and needs to be accounted for at the start of the project. The publisher will usually require the institution or the curator to raise the money for images.

Almost-aphorisms for the use of the guest curator

If I stress above the complexity of the processes of bringing an exhibition to completion, it is because they are difficult to unpick in a short overview. There is not space here to go into detail about the exhilarating mix of frustrations and rewards. Instead, I append some advice to help in finding a way through some of the challenges of being a guest curator.

♦ Exhibitions need foresight, forward planning, and room for revision. Everything takes longer than you think, so your schedule should include time for change, updates, and reassessments.

♦ The loan request process is long and sometimes frustrating and, in my experience, is rarely without hitches of various kinds – chiefly arising from the unavailability of works. Don't expect everything to go right, but be prepared to make compromises, and seek creative alternatives. In that way, when things do go to plan it will be a pleasant surprise.

♦ The installation process is both fascinating and engrossing but requires two qualities: patience and the ability to work closely and efficiently with teams of technicians.

♦ Exhibitions rely on team work. It is important not to take any of the team workers for granted. They have other work to do and other deadlines to meet, and will not thank you for creating unnecessary work.

♦ Always ask for advice from museum professionals in solving problems or seeking solutions. They will have appropriate experience in dealing with loans, insurance, and other aspects of the project with which you, as guest curator, are almost certainly not equipped to deal.

♦ Avoid getting the museum involved in complex, embarrassing, and possibly legal, issues by making promises to lenders or outside agents.

♦ Never seek to put pressure on private lenders, and always refer them to the institutional curators for advice about insurance and other formal arrangements. All loans are subject to certain limitations – some lenders will not permit their works to tour, for example, and you have to learn to accept their decision.

I hope your learning curve is just as steep as mine has been and that it affords just as rewarding a view when you finish the interesting climb!

Acknowledgements: My thanks to Victoria Osborne and her colleagues at Birmingham Museum and Art Gallery.

Curating 'Madness and Modernity'

Dr Leslie Topp

Co-curator of a major exhibition about mental illness and the visual arts in fin-de-siècle Vienna. Interviewed by Michael Davies

Madness and Modernity: Mental Illness and the Visual Arts in Vienna 1900, held at the Wellcome Collection, London, between 1 April and 28 June 2009, explored the myriad connections that existed in Vienna in the years 1890 to 1914 between psychiatry and mental illness on the one hand, and progressive visual arts (including architecture, design, drawing, and painting) on the other. It was curated by Leslie Topp (Birkbeck) and Gemma Blackshaw (University of Plymouth). A revised version of the exhibition, curated by Blackshaw and Sabine Wieber (University of Glasgow), was mounted at the Wien Museum, Vienna in 2010.

Presented in six thematic sections, the exhibition made connections through surprising, but historically grounded, juxtapositions of objects: Wiener Werkstätte designs with large-scale therapeutic equipment; Egon Schiele self-portraits with images from medical journals; architectural drawings by Otto Wagner with wax heads of patients with neurological conditions, and so on. The show was comprised of about 80 objects borrowed from public and private collections and institutions in Austria, the USA, and the UK. It also included two films commissioned from artist-filmmaker David Bickerstaff.

MD: *When did you first have the idea of mounting an exhibition about Madness and Modernity?*

LT: I began thinking in a very preliminary way that it would be interesting to put together an exhibition on this theme (the links between mental illness, psychiatry, and the progressive visual arts in Vienna c.1900) around 2002. This was partly in reaction to an AAH conference session I chaired in 2001 on mental illness and the visual arts, in which Gemma Blackshaw gave a paper on Egon Schiele's self-portraits and contemporary photographs of psychiatrically ill men. I had been working for a few years on the connections between modern architecture and psychiatry in Vienna, and it occurred to me that an exhibition would be a good way to bring these two strands of inquiry together. The idea became much more definite when Gemma got involved, and we applied in 2003 for an AHRC project grant with the exhibition as a major outcome. The grant allowed us to put together a team to work on the exhibition, including Sabine Wieber as curatorial adviser and Nicky Imrie as researcher.

MD: *Why the Wellcome? What other institutions did you think might have been interested?*

LT: The Wellcome's mission, to explore the connections between medicine, health, art, and culture, fitted perfectly with the theme of the exhibition. We did approach several other more mainstream art institutions (including the Hayward) initially, since we felt the show was really 'about' art, and worried that it might be marginalised (and also that it would be very difficult to get big fine-art loans) if it was shown at a science or medicine museum. But, during the course of our work

Madness and Modernity, Wellcome Collection, installation view (© Wellcome Library, London).

on the exhibition, the Wellcome Trust opened its new spaces, and it became clear that they were taken seriously as an art institution, so our worries were unfounded.

MD: *What stage were you at with your idea when you first contacted the Wellcome?*

LT: We had preliminary discussions with the Wellcome in 2004, but didn't come back to them until 2005, when the plans for the exhibition were very well developed and we had a detailed proposal and loan list in place.

MD: *How did you present your ideas to the Wellcome? Which illustrations or suggestions for exhibits (if any) were the most successful in persuading the institution to come on board?*

LT: We presented our ideas in the form of an illustrated proposal, which consisted of an introduction, floor plan, and details of each section within the show. We also presented a 'wish list' that was divided into sections and gave details of the location of objects. A commentary on any contacts made so far with lenders, as well as an assessment of how likely it was that we would get the respective loans, was also provided at this early stage. I feel that the fact the proposal was well developed worked in our favour. Images of loan objects, and the clear and specific theme for the display were also important in persuading them. The Wellcome had provided us beforehand with a floor plan of the space, and we included a schematic plan for the exhibition in our proposal – at the same time making it clear that we were very open to ideas from the Wellcome curators and the exhibition designers.

MD: *How much input did you have in the design process? How did the finished exhibition compare with your initial concept?*

LT: The Wellcome solicited bids from external specialist exhibition designers (teams of 3D (architectural) and 2D (graphic) designers) for the exhibition design, and we had a significant say in the selection of the team that was eventually chosen. We then worked closely in a team with the two designers (Calum Storrie and Lucienne Roberts), the senior curator of the Wellcome (James Peto), and the Wellcome's exhibition coordinator (Jane Holmes), to refine the plans for the exhibition. The finished product was close to our initial concept – the main differences were the result of not being able to secure certain important loans. Collaboration with the designers went extremely well, and we both felt that their interventions improved the exhibition in several ways.

MD: *How long did the process take from start to finish? What changes or stages were necessary along the way?*

LT: It took seven years from the initial idea to the mounting of the exhibition. We revised our plans numerous times, especially in terms of the size of the exhibition, and the number of sections and objects – these revisions reflected changes in our thinking but also represented responses to the different missions, preferences, and physical facilities of the institutions to which we proposed the exhibition. So, for instance, we de-emphasised contextual objects (e.g. therapeutic machinery) in proposals to more conventional art venues, but stressed their importance in our proposal to the Wellcome.

MD: *How did you agree the allocation of responsibilities for the project between yourselves and the Wellcome?*

LT: The senior curator drew up a contract and consulted us on it – basically we were responsible for curatorial decisions, locating loan objects, drafting loan letters, and writing wall texts, as well as for taking part in the discussions already mentioned. The Wellcome were responsible for sending out the loan letters and following up on them, negotiating with lenders about insurance, transport, marketing, media relations, and for devising public programmes. We also agreed to be available for newspaper, radio, and TV interviews, and were given media training by the Wellcome.

It's worth mentioning too that the Wellcome wasn't particularly involved in producing the catalogue for the show. We were responsible for finding a publisher and producing the text and images, and some subvention was provided by the grant (with the Wellcome also pitching in a small sum of money).

MD: *How much was the overall budget for producing the exhibition?*

LT: I don't know – we left all this to the Wellcome. Other than the background research for the exhibition, which was funded by the AHRC grant, the Wellcome paid all the costs.

MD: *How did your fee operate – was it separated between research and curating/project management?*

LT: We were paid a flat fee.

MD: *What do you feel the process has taught you about initiating and curating future projects?*

LT: One of the main lessons I derived from the process was about the importance of getting curators from your preferred host institution involved from the outset. We were in the position of approaching potential host institutions as outsiders – academics with no museum affiliations – and this resulted in the long delay we experienced in pinning down a host institution.

The Role of the Exhibition Designer

Ivor Heal

Designer of temporary exhibitions and permanent installations for leading museums and galleries in the UK and abroad. Interviewed by Michael Davies

A professional exhibition designer can bring a range of creative skills to the process of producing an exhibition, from devising a simple exhibition layout to graphic design, lighting, and even helping select and position exhibits. How much or how little they will be involved will depend largely on the size and complexity of the exhibition and on the budget available. Their most important role is, however, as an interpreter who translates the story an academic or curator wants to tell into three-dimensional reality, and for this to work successfully there has to be a measure of trust on both sides. For an academic new to exhibiting, it is probably best to be guided by a museum or gallery in the selection of a suitable designer, either using an in-house designer, someone they have already worked with, or by a formal selection process.

MD: *What is the typical lead-in time for a project from initial discussions to the opening of a permanent installation or temporary exhibition?*

IH: In the case of a permanent installation it will vary from anything between two to five years. Most programmes require the longer time-frame, to allow for working with the client and curators, producing the design concepts, initial drawings, visuals, and measured drawings, prior to the issue of tenders for construction.

Aztecs Royal Academy of Arts, London, 2002 The Walpole Award for British Excellence 2003 (© Ivor Heal Design Ltd).

A temporary exhibition is driven much more by the deadline of an opening date, and fitting it into a prepared schedule of events. The lead-in varies between six and 18 months, depending on the size of the exhibition and whether the editorial concept and exhibit list is well advanced before our appointment as designers.

MD: *Are you always given a detailed brief, or do you sometimes have to draw one up yourself? If so, how do you set about it?*

IH: Some briefs are extremely detailed. Working with the National Gallery on the Stubbs exhibition, for example, the paintings and the works on paper were chosen by the curator, and their location within each gallery was generally pre-determined. In the case of the new Wedgwood Museum, the brief was essentially more simple – to tell the story of Wedgwood. Working closely with the editor and researcher, we devised a design concept that expanded the themes suggested by the Wedgwood collection, placing them in a wider historical context. These included the historical design movements, fashion traits, and commercial requirements that influenced the production of the Wedgwood company.

MD: *Who, typically, is your main contact throughout a project at a museum or gallery – the director, curator, academic researcher, or a committee? Who is the easiest to work with?*

IH: Often the curator and the researcher are one and the same person, having devised the concept and compiled the exhibit list. It is rare to work with a committee, although the curator or I will make presentations to them to review progress and discuss design issues. This would also apply to a director; although on occasions it is the director who has curated the exhibition.

A curator with experience of creating an exhibition is usually the easiest to work with. He or she will appreciate a designer's level of knowledge of a subject, and be prepared to spend time discussing it. I have been fortunate to work repeatedly with certain curators on a number of projects, and having common knowledge of a subject can make working together so much easier. Sometimes the ideas and concepts are quite complex; as a designer I need to find a way of presenting these in a comprehensible way to the public. It can be a long and difficult process to resolve, especially when dealing with science and technology.

MD: *What are the easy and difficult aspects of working with academics or art historians?*

IH: I trained and worked as a sculptor, and was subsequently Head of Design at the Victoria and Albert Museum. This experience has been invaluable when collaborating with academics and art historians – a working knowledge of a subject really helps the process. The expert frequently finds it difficult to reduce the scope of a subject to suit the layout and size of the galleries. If not resolved, this could result in a very crowded design.

MD: *Which of your projects had the smallest budget and which the largest?*

IH: A budget is usually set relative to the size of the project, but sometimes it is very small compared to the brief. The smallest budget recently was for the Royal Gallery in the Houses of Parliament, where a series of changing exhibitions could utilise existing showcases and lighting.

In 1985, we were commissioned to redesign the American National Museum of Racing and Hall of Fame in Saratoga Springs, New York. With a budget in excess of £6 million, the museum was completely refurbished, with new displays, audio-visual presentations, a new film theatre, auditorium, and entrance foyer.

MD: *As a designer in what way can you influence the theme of an exhibition?*

IH: Primarily through creating a sense of atmosphere, mood, or period. This can be done with the use of colour or 'set-building', to evoke a period or subject. Introducing film or large photographic images, with music or sound, can also influence the way a visitor understands a theme.

In the Aztec exhibition, at the Royal Academy, by positioning a sculpture of a single figure in a dark space, with steps rising up behind, the scene immediately evoked a sense of menace and power (*see previous page*). In another gallery, the layout and placing of the works followed the original layout of a temple precinct. Together with sloped walls and structures, a sense of rising up to the temple entrance was created, even though the visitor remained on one level.

MD: *Have you sometimes had to tone down one of your powerful designs for an exhibition for fear that it might overpower the exhibits?*

IH: My design philosophy is first and foremost to be guided by the exhibits themselves. They have priority, and are the reason the visitor comes to the show in the first place. A successful exhibition is one where the design presents the

China: The Three Emperors 1662–1795
Royal Academy of Arts, London, 2005
(© Ivor Heal Design Ltd).

work of art or exhibit in the best possible way and does not intrude on this experience. In The Three Emperors at the Royal Academy, there was an initial tendency for the 'set' concepts to be over-elaborate in detail. Fortunately this was corrected during the design stage.

MD: *Have you ever been asked to help a museum or gallery with making a proposal to potential sponsors? If so, what has this involved?*

IH: Yes I have. For a designer this will involve several tasks: the production of an outline scheme, with plans and elevations; a description of the design concept; images of the most important works for display and their editorial context. It is likely that an artist's impression or perspective of the finished scheme will be required. Finally, I might be asked to produce an estimated budget for the construction and installation of the exhibition or work.

MD: *How has the introduction of computers affected your work as a designer? And, has it made your job as a project manager easier?*

IH: For myself the work process has not changed; the computer is just an additional tool. My first thoughts are most easily expressed with pencil and paper. Perspective sketches, concepts of space or structure, notes and ideas can be visualised more quickly on paper than on a computer. They also have a sensitivity, which I prefer.

From these sketches and notes I develop more detailed drawings on paper before committing them to the computer. It is at this next stage that technology is extremely useful. Changes can be made instantly; the laborious repetition of hand-drawn plans and elevations is avoided; the finished drawing can be sent instantly to others for comment; and the final printing can be completed in my studio.

For project management, communication using email is now more efficient and reliable.

MD: *Which of your permanent installations are you most proud of, and which temporary exhibition, and why?*

IH: Most recently the new permanent Wedgwood Museum at Barlaston near Stoke-on-Trent, which won the 2009 Art Fund Prize (previously the Museum of the Year Award). The museum covered several centuries of design, told the story of one man of genius, and displayed several thousand exhibits. The project lasted several years, and as designer it is always extremely satisfying and rewarding to see the original concept remain relatively unchanged on completion.

The Van Gogh exhibition at the Royal Academy presented a notable challenge – to reveal a different aspect of the artist, as a great writer as well as a painter. The exhibits were small letter-sketches which were required to be shown in cases alongside the related work in oil. This needed sensitive lighting, meeting the needs of both the two elements, and careful design of the mounts for the letters. In many instances, the documents had to be seen from both sides which also proved challenging.

In 1999 it was rewarding to design the Van Dyck exhibition at the Koninklijk Museum in Antwerp. Working with the architect we were able to create new openings in the walls of the galleries which facilitated a better visitor route and therefore coherence to the exhibition. The result was an excellent example of architect, designer, and curator working well together to achieve the best result.

The wide range of exhibitions Ivor Heal has worked on, and the long-term working relationships he has developed with curators at major museums and galleries is testament to his skill as an exhibition designer. This has been founded on a well-informed and sensitive understanding of the brief given to him by academics and curators, who in turn have clearly had complete faith in his ability to translate this into a successful exhibition.

The Wedgwood Museum 2008, Wedgwood Museum Trust.
Winner of Museum of the Year 2009
(© Ivor Heal Design Ltd).

Relevant Funding Bodies

Funding may be sought from charitable trusts and foundations. A selection of such organisations is as follows:

Arts Council England (Grants for the Arts)
www.artscouncil.org.uk/funding/grants-arts

Association of Art Historians
www.aah.org.uk/page/3248

The Barns-Graham Charitable Trust
www.barns-grahamtrust.org.uk

British Academy
www.britac.ac.uk/funding/index.cfm

The Crafts Council
www.craftscouncil.org.uk

The Economic and Social Research Council
www.esrc.ac.uk/funding-and-guidance

Esmée Fairbairn Foundation
www.esmeefairbairn.org.uk/funding/index.html

The Leverhulme Trust
www.leverhulme.ac.uk/funding/funding.cfm

The Mark Fitch Fund
www.marcfitchfund.org.uk

The Paul Mellon Centre for Studies in British Art
www.paul-mellon-centre.ac.uk/11

Wingate Scholarships
www.wingatescholarships.org.uk

The Winston Churchill Memorial Trust
www.wcmt.org.uk

For further information visit the Museum and Exhibition Group's funding webpages: www.aah.org.uk/page/3285.

List compiled by Lucinda Middleton

Notes on Contributors

Heather Birchall worked as a Curatorial Assistant at the V&A in London before moving to Tate Britain as an Assistant Curator. At Tate she worked on the organisation and interpretation of large-scale exhibitions and displays, and researched matters relating to the acquisition and cataloguing of historic and contemporary British art. In April 2007 she moved to the Whitworth Art Gallery in Manchester as Curator (Historic Fine Art) where, until early 2011, she managed the collection of historic watercolours and prints, and supported the programme of fine art exhibitions. Heather is author of *The Pre-Raphaelites* (2010), and has contributed many catalogue pieces and journal articles as well as essays and other texts. She chaired the AAH Museums & Exhibitions Members Group Committee from 2007 until 2010.

Colin Cruise teaches at the School of Art, Aberystwyth University. He has published widely on 19th-century art, writing on Rossetti, Burne-Jones, Pater, and Wilde, among other subjects. He curated two major exhibitions: Love Revealed: Simeon Solomon and the Pre-Raphaelites (2005) and The Poetry of Drawing: Pre-Raphaelite Designs, Studies and Watercolours (2011), both of them for Birmingham Museum and Art Gallery. His book *Pre-Raphaelite Drawing* was published by Thames and Hudson in 2011. He is currently working on a research project on narrative forms in British art and visual culture.

Michael Davies completed an MA in History of Art and Architecture at Cambridge in 1968. He then set up in business in London, first as a freelance graphic designer. Then, in 1978, he formed his own exhibition design and contracting company, based in Putney. The company specialised in producing exhibition stands at trade fairs around the world for individual organisations and national government groups, such as Russia, Japan, Tanzania, and Peru. At the same time, it developed expertise in designing museums and temporary museum exhibitions. Mike's long-term aim had, however, always been to return to academic research. And so, in 2001, he scaled down his business and started studying part-time for a History of Art MA at Birkbeck, which he completed, with a distinction, in 2003. He is now studying, still at Birkbeck, for a PhD focusing on The 1851 Great Exhibition,

drawing on both his business experience and his academic training. Mike has been a member of the AAH Museums & Exhibitions Members' Group Committee since 2007.

Ivor Heal graduated from Bath Academy of Art with a BA (Hons) degree in Sculpture. In 1969, under Sir John Pope-Hennessy, he started the design department of the Victoria and Albert Museum. In 1978 he left to form his own company, specialising in museum and exhibition design. Working extensively both in the UK and abroad, he designed two horse-racing museums in America and Hong Kong, a Henry Moore retrospective in Madrid and for the British Museum he created the exhibition The Enduring Image, shown in Delhi and Mumbai. In the UK his major projects include those for the Manchester Museum (University of Manchester) and, more recently, the new Wedgwood Museum at Barlaston. For the Royal Academy he has designed over 50 exhibitions, notably Alberto Giacometti; Aztecs; Paris: Capital of the Arts; Russia: French and Russian master paintings; Rodin; and The Real Van Gogh. Ivor most recently designed Degas and the Ballet: Picturing Movement for the Royal Academy.

Catherine E. Karkov is Professor of Art History, Director of the Centre for Critical Studies in Museums, Galleries and Heritage, and Head of the School of Fine Art, History of Art and Cultural Studies at the University of Leeds. Her research focuses on the art of early medieval England from a postcolonial perspective. The Roman to English exhibition was developed in conjunction with the AHRC-funded Postcolonising the Medieval Image project.

Laura MacCulloch started working in art galleries as a volunteer at the Barber Institute of Fine Art during her undergraduate degree. In 2004 she won a paid internship at the Barber Institute, working for a year in the education, curatorial and, press and marketing departments. Whilst completing her collaborative PhD thesis on Birmingham Museums and Art Gallery's collection of works on paper by Ford Madox Brown, she co-curated the first major exhibition of his work since 1964, and co-authored the accompanying catalogue. During this time she also worked as assistant curatorial technician, hanging exhibitions and redisplays at the Barber Institute. She is now the Curator of British Art at National Museums Liverpool, and is responsible for the collections at the Walker Art Gallery, the Lady Lever Art Gallery and Sudley House. Before moving to Liverpool she wrote the entries for works by numerous artists, including Ford Madox Brown, Frederick Sandys, and William Dyce for Birmingham's award winning online Pre-Raphaelite Resource (www.preraphaelites.org). Laura has been a member of the Museums & Exhibitions Members Group Committee since 2007.

Lucinda Middleton spent eight years as Curator of Fine & Decorative Arts at the Royal Cornwall Museum, where she developed interests in Cornish fine art and ceramics. She produced a catalogue and exhibition of the Bryan Pearce Bequest which she secured for the collection. After putting on the first John Opie exhibition for over 30 years, her research interests moved to another Cornish artist, enameller Henry Bone and his dynasty, which she is currently researching independently with the assistance of a Paul Mellon Research Support Grant. She joined the committee of the Museums & Exhibitions Members Group in 2008, and helped instigate the Group's Bursary scheme.

Outi Remes is the Director of the New Ashgate Gallery, Surrey and the Adjunct Associate Professor in Art History and Visual Culture at Richmond, The American International University. She also lectures at Birkbeck College, the University of London, and worked as the Head of Exhibitions at South Hill Park Arts Centre, Berkshire (2007–11). She was awarded a PhD from the University of Reading (2005).

Leslie Topp is Senior Lecturer in the Department of History of Art and Screen Media at Birkbeck, University of London. Her work focuses on architecture, design, and urbanism in Central Europe in the early 20th century. She is author of *Architecture and Truth in Fin-de-Siècle Vienna* (Cambridge University Press, 2004) and co-editor of *Madness, Architecture and the Built Environment: Psychiatric Spaces in Historical Context* (Routledge, 2007).

Amelia Yeates is Lecturer in Art History at Liverpool Hope University, where she set up and now runs the MA Art History and Curating. She is a member of the AAH Museums & Exhibitions Members Group Committee, and works closely with museums and galleries in Liverpool, for example Tate Liverpool and National Museums Liverpool (NML). Her research interests are 19th-century British art and literature, and she teaches widely on 19th- and 20th-century art, as well as on museum studies.